INFORMATI ON PRODUCT CREATION IDEAS

Tips on creating your very own info product

Leon Rowe

TABLE OF CONTENTS

INTRODUCTION

The most frequently stated factor in startup failure is a lack of market demand. However, there will always be a demand for information on the market. The mere existence of Google Search proves that there is a genuine demand for it. Information products are not only in high demand, but they are also among the simplest to market. So why not start with the most obvious option—information products—if you're an aspiring entrepreneur, creative, or hobbyist trying to make passive income?. In this book, you'll get ideas on getting your own info product out there. So, read on to find out how to make money selling information products and earn passive income.

CHAPTER 1

WHAT IS AN INFORMATION PRODUCT?

Any piece of information or instruction that aids someone in learning something new is considered an info product.

It might be a tool that teaches people more about who they are, how to strike the elusive work-life balance, or how to set and meet goals.

It could include instruction on how to increase their chances of finding employment, how to attract more clients, how to earn money online, how to start a profitable blog, how to create a website, etc. Aside from these topics, info goods also go over how to make videos, sell your own services, become a freelancer, write website copy, and other related topics.

Your options for themes to base your knowledge product on are virtually endless. However, did you realize that not all information products need to be digital assets of some sort?

You can design information items where you personally impart training, that's correct.

One example of a non-digital information product is coaching or mentoring. Live occasions like webinars and seminars are another option. Info products can be used to generate income in a variety of ways without going digital initially. To build information products, you do not require any specialized knowledge. Actually, the majority of those who do earn money from selling them aren't very talented writers or marketers; instead, they just use pre-existing content and repurpose it into something unique and useful that meets a need for their audience and community.

By creating your own information product, you can have complete control over the process. Everything is up to you, from selecting the subject to crafting the copy. For your information product to begin, you must have some sort of notion or idea.

Making and ensuring your information product is something people will find beneficial is the most crucial aspect of marketing it. If they don't require what you offer, they won't be very interested in purchasing from you.

Asking them directly is the greatest method to learn if they require what you provide. This could be from study into your area of expertise and what people are interested in learning more about, or it could just result from simply generating ideas with friends or coworkers.

When you have this basic idea in mind, you should consider the best way to communicate it.

CHAPTER 2

TIP 1 – ORGANIZE A VIRTUAL EVENT

A virtual event frequently features multiple speakers. The ability to present a virtual event live and for free in order to attract opt-ins is one of its coolest features.

The recordings can then be afterwards sold as a collection of video courses.

Your opt-in and upsell are effectively baked into the cake as a result of this. To put it another way, you only need to design one product in order to establish a whole sales funnel around it. Although that is a really effective paradigm, there are other methods to implement this. You can, for instance:

Sell tickets to the multiple-day event on your website and social media pages.

• Provide a VIP ticket that allows attendees to access Q&As following the session.

Following the virtual event, you can repackage and sell that.

You have the choice to build a program on your membership sites that includes these sessions if you've participated in a lot of these virtual events.

Alternately, you might compile the greatest concepts from the virtual event into an eBook.

Once more, you can always change up how you produce and advertise these goods.

CHAPTER 3

TIP 2 – USE A PORTION OF AN EXISTING PRODUCT

This strategy's goal is to take one of your current goods, extract out a section of it, and then sell this fragmented section separately or use it as a lead magnet.

I'll give you a few instances:
• You have a video course on kettlebell training. One video module is split out and sold separately.

• You've written an eBook about organic gardening. You take a chapter on identifying and treating plant diseases, excerpt it, and then market this report as a tripwire item.

• You are taking a self-paced course on generating online traffic. The element of the training that is devoted to social media marketing is split out and sold separately.

This is another really quick method of producing a new good. The fact that the fragmented product will inevitably lead to the main product is one of the key advantages, nevertheless. And in doing so, you're producing a good with a potential for backend sales.

CHAPTER 4

TIP 3 – SEEK THE SERVICES OF AN EXPERT

You can still save time and money by paying someone to perform some of the research if you don't want to engage someone to design the complete product. In this situation, you might explain to your freelancer what you're looking for before giving them the reins to conduct the necessary research and outline. You're developing a product around social networking, for instance. You may ask your freelancer to gather data on the number of users on various social media platforms and the demographics of the audiences you can expect to find there.

• You are producing a gardening item. In order to manage pests and diseases that are specific to each region, you can hire someone to conduct study on the various parts of the nation.

CHAPTER 5

TIP 4 – INTEGRATE PREVIOUSLY CREATED CONTENTS

You probably have a ton of content if you've been in business for a while. This covers blog articles, newsletters, social media posts, forum entries you've written as a guest blogger, and more.

It only takes a few seconds to combine many existing parts to quickly create something altogether new. This is still preferable to starting from scratch, even if you do need to make some adjustments to make them work together.

You can:

- Create a report by compiling several blog entries. To make it read more smoothly, you might need to add introductions and transitions between posts.
  Alternately, mention that this is a collection of your best posts to the readers.
- Compile numerous articles and reports to produce an eBook. Although you will once more need to make transitions, this method is quicker than starting from scratch.

- Convert a digital good (such an eBook) into a tangible one. Even if you don't provide value in other ways, this raises the product's perceived value.

- Convert a text-based product into a video-based one, or the other way around. This is an additional strategy for raising a product's perceived worth.

CONCLUSION

The amount of time required to produce many things is not much. The alternative is to simply exercise some imagination. When you use the aforementioned advice, you'll be able to create things quicker and more easily than you ever imagined. You may have a new product ready to market today if you put these techniques to use right now. The important thing is that the product provide value and responds to the customer's request. You will succeed regardless of the thing you are actually selling if you sincerely assist people in transforming their lives by helping them with their difficulties. One or two of these information product ideas are always a good place to start, and from there you may expand while continuing to build your company little by little. Recurring income, geographic independence, and a lifestyle that is challenging to maintain in any other way come once you've discovered that knowledge niche.